C A L I F O R N I A   P O E T R Y   S E R I E S

5

Priscilla Lee

# WISHBONE

THE ROUNDHOUSE PRESS

Publisher's Cataloging-in-Publication Data
Lee, Priscilla, 1966–
    Wishbone / Priscilla Lee
            p. cm. — (California poetry series ; v. 5)
    ISBN: 0-9666691-4-2
    1.   Asian American women — Poetry   2. I. Title.
    PS3562.E359 W57 2000
    811'.6 — dc21                                                      00-008264

Grateful acknowledgment is made to the editors of the following journals and anthologies in which versions of these poems first appeared: *Alaska Quarterly Review, Another Chicago Magazine, BAKUNIN, Barrow Street, Berkeley Poetry Review, The Cafe Review, The Cream City Review, Gargoyle, The Kenyon Review, Konch, The Mid-American Review, Phoebe, Ploughshares, Poetry Flash, Rain City Review, The San Francisco Bay Guardian, Urban Spaghetti, ZYZZYVA, ModernWife.com, Making More Waves: New Writing by Asian American Women,* and *Storming Heaven's Gate: An Anthology of Women's Spiritual Writing.*

I wish to thank the San Francisco Foundation for their James D. Phelan Literary Award. "Shaman" received the 1996 Greg Grummer Award in Poetry from *Phoebe: A Journal of Literary Arts.* This book was written with the encouragement and support of many wonderful people to whom I extend my deepest thanks: Robert Evans, Liz Dossa, Maureen Crisick, Thea Sullivan, Kim Addonizio, Yvonne Cannon, Helen Wickes, Noah Blaustein, Forrest Hamer, Karen Lee Hones, Ina Campbell, Nan Breedlove, Jay Moores, Joyce Jenkins, Patricia Wakida, Malcolm Margolin, my husband, George Ripley, and my family.

This is Volume 5 of the California Poetry Series.
Cover: Anonymous Kuan Yin painting on glass, Rick Mariani Photography
Author Photo: Katya Kallsen
Cover and Interior Design: David Bullen Design

The California Poetry Series is published by The Roundhouse Press and distributed by Heyday Books. It is available directly from Heyday Books, or through Small Press Distribution and other wholesalers.

Subscription orders, inquiries, and correspondence should be addressed to:
Heyday Books
P.O. Box 9145
Berkeley, California 94709
phone: 510.549.3564  fax: 510.549.1889
e-mail: roundhouse@heydaybooks.com
www.heydaybooks.com

Printed in Canada
10   9   8   7   6   5   4   3   2   1

# Contents

*For Grandma & my husband, George*

"But you know, grandson, this world is fragile." The word he chose to express "fragile" was filled with the intricacies of the continuing process, and with a strength inherent in spider webs woven across paths through sand hills where early in the morning the sun becomes entangled in each filament of web. It took a long time to explain the fragility and intricacy because no word exists alone, and the reason for choosing each word had to be explained with a story about why it must be said this certain way. That was the responsibility that went with being human, old Ku'oosh said, the story behind each word must be told so there could be no mistake in the meaning of what had been said; and this demanded great patience and love.

Leslie Marmon Silko, from *Ceremony*

## The Vision

In my room, Kuan Yin guards my bed.
*Goddess of Unmarried Women.*
*Goddess of Fertility.*
*Goddess of Mercy.*
She stands on a throne of gold-tipped lotus,
holding a white horsetail duster
and metal rings to encircle
the heads of the disobedient.

Her black hair flows over her white veils,
and she smiles to me as her pink lotus flies
across the sky. Sometimes she carries
an infant in her arms,
but Kuan Yin is not the Virgin Mary.
The child she carries is not her own.

I have prayed to her since I was a child
before I knew what prayer meant,
when daily my mother slapped
the bamboo stick across my arms and legs,
and my prayers became the bridge across the pain.

My grandmother tells me to release my childhood,
remember only that Kuan Yin plucked me off
the wobbly junk of a boat gypsy
and flew me to her,
dark orphan, my skin rashed and peeling.

Today, walking through the streets of Chinatown
I buy images of her.
Sometimes pewter, sometimes bargain jade,
these small comforts
I collect like tokens
to buy my way across.

## Portsmouth Square, 1966

In the picture, I am nine months old,
tight white
bundle in red booties
carried out for a walk in the park. You are a thin
fortyish woman in cat-eye glasses
and a blue chemise,
young enough to be my mother.
You were the one who woke before dawn
to feed me, and the one who now waits
for me by the window in the evenings.

My mother and I were the packaged deal
you sent for: Hong Kong bride with child on the way,
the marriage that would save
your oldest son from Vietnam.

So, when my mother arrived
in this country, hunch-shouldered
and sway-backed, her five-month pregnancy hidden
under a small beaded sweater, you boiled
angelica root and whole chickens for soup,
and promised to bring her mother and sisters
to America. Later, after she complained
that the constant crying tore at her heart,
you moved me into your room
across the hall, tied me
down to the crib with rope.

In this picture, I did not know
who my mother was. I will not know until
almost three years later, dragging
a blanket from our room,
I see a beautiful woman in floral pajamas,
bending over to light
the furnace in the hallway, her powdered face
glowing from the flame. I will ask you
who the woman is, and you will answer,
she is your mother.

## Prayers to Buddha

*You are the sun that rises above water*
*the jade buried in stone*
*a woman who gives birth to sons*

My grandmother reads
from the almanac of life
tucked under my bed
since the year I was born.

I am the gypsy child she raised,
more important
than her own children,
I cannot be labeled by a number.

For me she lights incense daily,
picks one Chinese character
and counts two rounds of five fingertips
until her eyebrows no longer twitch
and she knows

I am safe from men
with heads but no tails
who want to draw
circles with their right hand
squares with their left.

These men, she says,
can only pray to Buddha
for salvation, journey through snow
in thin-soled shoes, cross
the mud-bridge.
They cannot offer the life
her prophesy commands.

## Midwife

Sunday night in the living room
my grandmother reads *The Chinese Times*
with a cracked magnifying glass
and one lamp. She does this every Sunday
when my mother and the other children
are not around, and I lie on the couch,
quiet so as not to disturb her contemplation.
Today, she will think back to a time
in China, when at eighteen,
delicate, useless for the village,
she is married off
to a country herb doctor.

In his village, she could not carry
a child in her arms and two buckets
of water from her shoulders,
did not know how to walk
through a rice field without slippers.
But she delivered children, house to house,
even after she had seen her brother-in-law
kneel on broken glass, and beaten
so brutally with a steel rod, that afterwards,
he hanged himself from an iron gate,
or even after she had heard the news
that two evenings before, during a curfew,
a Japanese soldier had shot a pregnant woman
crawling across a wide dirt road
because he thought she was a pig.

The babies, hard births—
the urine, blood, and waste
so thick on sheets, she had to smoke
to keep from retching—
she delivered for a bunch of dried vegetables,
a bag of rice, even nothing.

## Wishbone

In the bedroom, the old Chinese sisters, my grandmother
and great-aunt, are shoving their folded dollars
into lucky red envelopes all morning.
My great-aunt is visiting from Canada,
widowed fifty years, and her only child,
a baby girl without hair, was found
dead one night, overfed
by the maid. My grandmother, the younger sister,
fills her house in America
with four children and eleven grandchildren,
complains about dying
every weekend.

Forty years, few facts
have changed, yet they are arguing relentlessly
again as they wait for my youngest uncle
to take them out for Sunday dim sum, the little bit
of heart over tea. *You carried your son to me, piggyback.*
No, my son was old enough to walk.
*You gave your son to me, then you took him back.*
No, you told him my village was full of cow dung
so he wouldn't come back.

In my family, this is our legacy.
Every generation, a child is given away for safekeeping
because of war, poverty, other children.
My mother gave me
to my grandmother, and I was twelve
when my youngest uncle told me
*Respect your mother because she has lost.*
*If she and your grandmother were drowning,*
*we know whose life you would save.*

When the morning arguing boils off,
and every red envelope in the house is filled,
my uncle arrives, and the family stands back
as the two sisters push towards him
like knives over his heart.

## Fruits

Sometimes when we sit in the living room
my mother tells us how much she misses
the plums and mangoes she ate in China.

When she was a young woman,
she sliced cadavers at the clinics and practiced
puncturing ear lobes, wrists, and temples.
She wasn't afraid of anything, never missed home,
wandered with her backpack, her girlfriends,
barefoot on dirt roads, eating.

She was a big girl with thick pigtails
and a high nose. My father carries pictures
in his wallet, says she is almost Russian.
She swam so much, had such wide shoulders.

Nothing is said about why she escaped
to Hong Kong, married my father, the fat boy
she made fun of in school.
Nothing about why she gave me
to my grandmother or the children
she tried to have later, but lost.
She talks about the plums and mangoes
she remembers to be sweeter than here.

Once when I was sixteen, she took me aside,
told me she knew the kind of woman
I would become. I would want it all,
but in middle-age, everything
would be tiring. I wouldn't think about sex,
she said as she closed her robe, walked
to the kitchen to boil the water.

## Family Dinner

My mother the hard boned
Chinese woman 23 years
in this country
without bothering to learn
its language
buys lean pork ribs
special order
at the Hop Sang in Chinatown
and cooks dinner
for an extended family
of twenty-five during holidays.

Seated loosely around
the dining table
trying to eat quietly
I am scrubbed down
to skin and bone,
her oldest daughter—
spineless, a headless snake
a woman grandfather says
who should have her tendons
lifted out slowly
by the steel point
of a darning needle
until she writhes.

To my mother
I'm useless
but dangerous,
capable of swallowing
the family whole
into my pelvis
while I sit
waiting for the boyfriend
white and forbidden
to touch our doorbell.

## Pretty Woman

she's Asian
in a different way

ex-Asian
in thigh high boots
and leather
just short enough
to give
the pinched nerve walk

down Stockton street
every corner
the odor rising
of urine and fish

she shifts
from roadside stand
to roadside stand, avoids
the swarm of eyes.

growing up
grandmother had said
white men can't tell
*good looking*
in a Chinese girl.

mother said
she is pretty
enough
to hang from a pole

and sell on streets.

## A Granddaughter's Obligations

At the Chinese Hospital
opposite Hang Seng
Fish Market on Jackson Street,
I visit my grandmother
almost daily. The oldest daughter
of her oldest daughter,
I am obligated. I bring the pork
and oiled lettuce leaves
over rice, another tin box
of salted crackers
for her hot water.

Cancer has swollen
her stomach, and she
does not want the milk
and meat loaf
the hospital serves.

When I see her,
my tongue flutters
its tenuous string
of 13 tones, sounds
you expect only
in a baby's
tight cries. "Ah Pah,
have you eaten
yet? You look
better. Today
not so pale
like yesterday.
Yesterday like
bamboo shoot
so pale."

She smiles, tells me
she is old and will not live
to see me married.

## Corner

The man in the quiet corner
of the living room, sits
completely blind, his weight dense,
stubborn flesh on a chair. My grandfather
has grown older, only reaches into darkness,
his voice exploding
every minute
into a shapeless room when he asks
for something simple, his eyedrops, a cup of hot water,
an extra custard tart, afraid now of death
in the same measure
he is afraid of an hour without urinating,
a day without bowel movements.
Nothing reassures him, not the tiny pills, the handful
of shelled walnuts, the warm bowl of oatmeal
we place in his hands. At night, I hear him
telling my grandmother
that the children
are taking him to the bathroom in a forest
somewhere in China. He feels the familiar cold, can hear
the wind and snapped branches rumbling
through the narrow hallway he shuffles along. He is fearful
he may catch pneumonia, wants them
to take him back into the house instead.

# Rain

No one remembers exactly
when my grandmother went crazy. Her thoughts
rattle like seeds inside an old melon
as she walks through the house
at night, fingertips pressing the soft top
of her skull. *The young man*
*at the doctor's office this morning*
*is the right age. He had parents she delivered*
*in China. The girl at the restaurant*
*must be a granddaughter of a classmate,*
*the one who escaped to Sydney.*

She may have gone crazy as a young woman
at the border between China
and Macau, four children and herself
waiting in a white room for the officer
to stamp their false passports:
firing squad and America
a telegram apart. She had kneeled
and prayed for rain.

Maybe it was down in Hong Kong,
the grey matchbox apartment for five,
the afternoon smell of soup bones
and decomposed fish on perpetual simmer.
No one recognized her
at the market, the stylish woman
in a long slip dress who bought up
the ginger and tiger balm and told peddlers
she was a midwife, delivered hundreds
at her village clinic. The migraines began then.
Her children remembered
the nights she crawled from bed
and asked them to run
the bathwater, her hands
dripping with sweat.

## What My Grandfather Sang

When the house is empty, the rooms fill
with his voice, drifting in
like air conditioning. *Walk to the corner*
*of the street, pick up an orange.*
He is singing his life. He sang when I was a child
to soothe me back to sleep. I used to watch
the night-light flicker, his silhouette resting
against the beige burlap drapes
as he pulled on his trousers.
*The streets are good. The orange sweet.*
The sun wasn't up yet, but it didn't matter—
he was going blind, could only see
the unsettled blur of cups
and counter on the days he worked.

I've seen the half dollar stuck
between his teeth, watched them close
the bronze casket lined with wool blankets,
the black satin wreath and paper money burning
into the afterlife. Now, his picture is suspended
in the corner of the dining room,
smiling over the altar. His blind eyes
watching over our every meal.

When the house is empty, I can hear
the wood creak beneath the rug,
his heavy footsteps, the slap and shuffle
of leather slippers sticking to tile,
when he walks into the kitchen.
*The streets are good. The orange sweet.*
I wonder when it will pass,
when I will stop sitting up alone at night
to keep this old man around me,
wanting his song, his voice to stretch
into every empty room I walk through,
wanting him to finally see me when he sings.

## 1522 Mason Street, San Francisco, 1969

Years later, I still hear the continuous
steel cable, vibrating in the groove
under Mason Street, Uncle Gary sobbing
because someone at the Laundromat stole
my diapers, his room pulsing with nervous music.
No one told me he left home until the day
I scuttled from the smack of my mother's slipper,
& she dragged me from under his empty bed.

I think of Grandma praying faster,
me looking under her skirt while she lit
offerings to our ancestors, her thick legs
rough with veins, the beige stockings sagging
under the pull of garters. She always loved me best,
since Uncle Gary hitchhiked East to study teeth.
Sometimes, when no one was home & you could hear
the crackling of mah jong tiles shuffled next door,
Grandma, Grandpa, & I watched strippers on TV.
I remembered Grandpa saying, "American women
will do anything" while the melon-breasted blonde
with a face like Kim Novak, pulled a feather boa
back & forth across her bottom.

I can remember the night Uncle Gary choked
on a fishbone because he didn't learn to eat
his fish heads right, Auntie Joyce poured vinegar
down his throat to make him throw up,
& Uncle Lealand hurled his chopsticks, chipping a plate
because the baby wouldn't stop wailing.
No one told the landlady we had ten people
crammed into three rooms or that Great Grandma
smoked & slept in the hall closet.
That night, Grandpa, blind & bulging with irritation,
flung the radio into the clanging cold.

## Empathy

### 1

He's not a smooth talker,
his voice sands the curve
of your inner ear like
coarse rolled oats, and
his arrogance grates
on you until your
tongue, laden with
heavy contempt
finally snaps back

*yet*
*he will know you*
*in an hour*
*you'll trust him*
*in half a day*
*he's a mind reader*
*he can read*
*your mind.*

### 2

He has been
an outsider
even before
he could spell
his own name, the
neurotic offspring of
two psychologists, they
buried a black box
of shed beliefs
deep into the small grey

folds of his mind.

The day he dosed
on acid at seventeen, he
crossed over
some barrier in
the mind; plodding through
the scurry of downtown
shoppers, he suddenly
watched as his
protective walls of
black lowered—
slowly, and his vision
sharpening, until
he was able to
see through the people
as if their outlines
were etched in emotion.


### 3

*he can*
*help you*
*he knows*
*how*
*you feel*

Now
sitting cross-legged
on the coffee table, as
you talk, he straightens
his spine; his head
rising to listen for
reverberations from
the system you've
painfully constructed
since childhood
to bridge
one day to one day.

A pause and he pries
through bone,
tunneling deep into
the maze
of blocked channels
with directed questions,
until your mind's
dark walls draw back,
dilapidating as you
spill outside
yourself.

*he has*
*helped you*

## Control

In lab
cervical cancer
cells of Henrietta Lacks
(she died
more than fifty years ago)
are incubated and
dividing
in a solution
vulnerable
to contamination. He wants
conditions to remain
sterile, switches
the lights off,
and returns home
to make love
to a sock between
a mattress and box springs.

## Lines

All night from a balcony she watches
Stephen walk down the street

and lengthen into other people. *Why
doesn't he stop by?*

The first time, Stephen told her a line
was like a thread and to pull

the speed until she felt the tip
of a needle piercing an eyebrow;

then, she'd know she drew the whole
line in. After the hospital,

she licks the dust off
mirrors just to be sure.

## Two People

Grandma gave me Lulu when I was five
and tired of life. Old Chinese women
in the Fillmore apartments thought I was crazy,
the buzzcut girl hauling a raggedy doll
to the bathroom and back, red stringy curls
sweeping the floor.

Lulu saw everything that happened,
her round eyes never closed. She told me
how the men held down my sister's thighs
so the needle wouldn't snap,
and later she saw Ma pushing sugar
into her drooling mouth. She told me
how the mice tunnel through soft white cheese
when I sleep.

Next door, Mimi's Ma smacked her
when she dropped her rice bowl. Ma said
she was a *HA*. Mimi cried
until she couldn't breathe right.
We were short stubs, eating
in jammie pants, my dark blue
bruise much prettier than hers.

In my dreams, women scratch the door
with their knotted fingers, dying
on the other side. *Why do you sleep so much?*
they call. I tell them I want to go home.

Now, Lulu crawls out of her cubby hole
when I am sad. We walk around the old rooms.
She cries a lot, doesn't want to grow up.
Sometimes she weighs so much
I don't get out of bed.
I feel like two people.
One of us has to carry the other.

## Blue Octopus

I told Grandma the octopus
is swimming in the toilet. It is blue
and watery, fills the toilet full.

Ma is not home. I feed it
Ex-lax, throw in Kleenex,
throw in bananas.

Grandma goes in
the bathroom. Comes out
Kleenex wrapped around
her fingers.

The octopus bit her.
There are blue teethmarks
under her fingernails.

## Offering

Grandmother peels the pale pulp from grapefruits, leaves
their bitter skin curled on a bone dish. I want to give my lover
Kuan Yin's statue. My small mosquito, the rock and roll star
in black high-tops, promised me a shrine, red candles,
perfume, and dried champak flowers for the altar. *Do not tear*
*your heart to feed a man. He will devour it as if it were*
*the lungs of a dog.* Grandmother sets the figure by the dish.
*Kuan Yin is not given as a gesture, even her name is holier*
*than the ocean's thunder. Why do you want to give him*
*this blessing?* She faces the statue toward me. *His nose*
*is like a knife. He will have a short life, eating wind and*
*coughing up bitterness.* She tells me a story: a boat girl brings
a Kuan Yin for her prospective husband, but he sends her away,
offended by the bribe. The girl leaves the statue to the beautiful
innkeeper. Years pass, and one day, when tossing fortune sticks
on the bodhisattva's birthday, the innkeeper meets the girl's
betrothed. *The Kuan Yin watches over their big plump sons.*
*Who will watch after you?* Grandmother asks, rubbing
the grapefruit skin over Kuan Yin and each petal of the lotus
she stands on, opening its center to light.

## Wane

Dense gray evening when breath moves
like cigarette smoke,
the disheveled baker tells the woman,
love ruins people, his voice tearing
as if a slice of bruschetta
scraped against his throat. He wants her
to get in his bed, holds one lame hand towards her,
and she takes the gloved dead wood,
because playing it safe is about the most dangerous
thing a woman like her could do.

My VCR flickers the time while Bella Luna shines
her face on the people of Brooklyn.
The luminous moon bringing the woman to the man.
Puccini's crescendos giving way
to the body. How love can ruin us.

Last winter in bed, you played me
your music box. Notes from its broken teeth
tangling in dry cold, you opened the drawers:
heads of red roses, a mink claw
resting on velvet. On the lid,
you had written, Pet—animal kept
for pleasure rather than utility.
I told you I knew what you meant,
an animal chews off its paw
to escape the trap.

I think of myself now, my moon always waning,
the shots of whiskey filling beer glasses.
You leave messages:
it has been cold and lonely,
your girlfriend, the woman you left me for,
in a different state. In dreams I beat you,
my rings catching your skin,
the blood on my palms, your hands
pushing my face. Sometimes I dream

I am in bed with a new lover,
but when I offer myself, I turn
into a five year old child, sex
small as a clam.

## Beast

Every weekend you drive 25 miles from Belmont
to my house in a '72 Plymouth Duster. We can do anything:
see a Zhang Yimou movie, heavy-handed in all
its sadness and revenge, sit in a large cafe
with hardly any people, or drink Tequila
Sunrises at the Embers while we watch old women
open their beaded clinch purses
and slap down tips on the counter
as if it were the late fifties. On weekends
we try for solace.

You say not having sex is like a jail sentence.
After she left, you paced all day
until only the bones held your skin up. You thought
you must be kidding yourself
because you weren't crying all the time.
Last night while you were floating
on the waterbed, a tall skinny man
who wore a white hospital smock
stood wailing by a wrought iron bed
in the corner of the room. The doctors broke into your dream,
shot him with medicine while you sat
and watched, occasionally tossing a soft toy
to distract his shrieking. Nothing made him better.
You tell me this man is you.

I say I don't care about sex, haven't forgotten
the sense of being gutted underwater, the nights
drinking refrigerated vodka after this lover left me.
I tell you about my dreams of men in rooms, the towels
wrapped around their waists, how I move from room
to room in a terry robe, do not touch them, want only
to find a bathroom where I can wash myself. In the hallway,
my grandmother looks into a mirror, tries to split an eyelash
with a razor blade. She does not see me.
Under the dim light, she is thinking
about the funeral, about breaking

the thick blue comb, and throwing the short half
into my grandfather's coffin, the long half
over the roof so he doesn't take her with him.
I tell you I am praying for our salvation.

## Nocturne

The blonde boy and the olive girl
are at the bar. Saturday night
at the Noc Noc and they are joking.
Beefeater doubled over
ice and she mentions
toys, dinosaurs. He answers
all the dildos in the sock drawer. Decapitated.
The batteries. Recycled. In household
appliances. Egg beaters. Chainsaws. They think
that this is funny. World hunger
is definitely his fault. They laugh.
Order another. This time
no ice. No lasagna. No potatoes.
They don't feel empty. They are not
suburban or middle-classed.
They are happy together.

You're the Christ figure, she says. He nods.
The rock and roll star. Like Jesus
leading millions. She's the martyr.
Her face like Buddha. He tells her
she is beautiful. Luminous
in the blue neon.

It won't happen. She promises. Kisses
his arm. The blond hair glistening.
The gold in dirt. No knife. No
twist. She knows she could, but God.
Karma. Each time she doesn't try,
doesn't succeed, the pain would lessen.
This time, it's tequila. Gold. Double.
The bartender says whatever.

They think they're empaths. Can-openers
puncturing people, the world filtering
blood in their bodies. She says she loves him.
He turns. Kisses her. Feels her heart. Clutch.

Fist. Then fingernails
digging into soft palm.
For a second, his eyes
cannot rotate.

## Down

*on the night we found out that Victor died*


Thursday no cover
at the Bench & Bar. We order
two, rag about Leslie
the neon lumberjack, folding shirts
at Berkeley Beach, who doesn't know
he's screaming, bitch about Ronnie
lounging in a mink stole growling *girrrl*
as if he had a lover in his boot, and when Chubby
with the horse habit croons *I know you're wrong
you're not that strong,* his falsetto
stretching to a plead, we suck our salted limes,
a bunch of losers wailing in our beers,
no longer chickens 'cause we know *that girl* can sing.

## Her Game

At the market a suit gives her
the once over as if she were
an ad for genuine draft.
When he makes the move
she'll insist on at least
a four star joint. She won't
care if he's new in town
or only wants to fuck—
straight up, no chaser because
if men look they might as well
pay and she been known
to pick up and book out,
leaving behind the doggie
bag and a note on their tab
that sex just isn't worth
the bother.

## Chinese Girl in the Mirror

### 1

English Class:
"You have a distinctly
Asian voice in your writing—
it's really quite
pleasant; maybe you should
write about the cross-
cultural experience."

### 2

At the store
Luzi says, "we had a routine check
by an undercover shopper
and we did well except
the short Oriental girl
talked with another employee."

What short Oriental girl?

### 3

I had lunch at Jun May Guey
loaded my best friend's bowl full
with tendons and
knotted intestines
every five minutes

He felt sick
I felt insulted

"Your idea of beef stew
is a couple pieces of meat
and a few wimpy carrots —hey,
we throw
the whole cow in!"

### 4

David, I only have
huge front teeth
because of evolution.
Through the ages, huge front teeth
have been selected for in Chinese
because China had few animals
to kill for food.
China being
a poor country

my ancestors ate
whatever vegetation
they found.

My teeth are for the purpose
of chewing bamboo shoots
and eating bark off trees.

### 5

Jack even asked me
whether my family would consider
going back to China
if the communists
were overthrown.

I told him
some of my family
could've been here longer
than his—
my great grandfather came
to build the railroads

and what did his
family ever do
to make him feel
more American than me.

## North Beach, 1993

At Caffe Greco, I lean my head against your arm while you
spread one hand over mine, stroke my cheek with your other.
You are more pink than me, show an outdoor flush
when you step indoors from the cold. I am more pale,
my skin translucent with olive undertones. I am not
yellow, my eyes are not almond-shaped, I was born in
America, so what marks me as Asian intrigues you, though
you can almost understand this distinction. You are Jewish,
a person born into a nation of tribes, scattered throughout
the world, but sitting at the table with your Earl Grey tea,
you don't look different than the other Americans at the cafe,
who can be Italian, Irish, or German, in their faded jeans
and bomber jackets. America is a unique country, you say.
If you are born here, you are an American. In no other place
can you assimilate so readily: a European born in China
wouldn't be Chinese, and the passport of a Jew, whose
family had been in Russia for a thousand years, would say
he is Jewish.

## Breaking

He is a soft quiet man. The butter
under my tongue, sometimes the sweet cream.
He is beautiful in his silent waverings
through most Sundays, distracted by the way
eucalyptus trees hold the flood of sunlight
from his eyes, or the way
lightning flashes blue across his window
before the thunder drives into the ocean,
or the way a wave pauses on sand.
*I don't know*
*whether to take you to Santa Cruz for the weekend*
*or to leave you.*

We tried to catch sandcrabs once:
the water draining between our fingers,
the wet sand in our cupped palms
after the waves have broken.
He told me he used to do this
as a child in Laguna Beach—sliding
the sandcrabs onto the hard ground and watching
their tiny legs
*run away, run away*
towards the water and softer sand.
*I can't leave you*
*because I love you.*

In the middle of the night, he calls for me
to hold him,
and I want to hold him to my chest
so he doesn't melt into the sheets
or disappear into the skylight where he keeps
the moon, his saucer of milk, for me.
*I love you, but*
*I'm not in love with you.*

All night we sleep, his inner thigh
wrapped around my hipbone, because he dreams
I am killed by a shower of meteors
and he cannot wrap his arms around me
when I disintegrate into a million stars.

# Palms

It is past noon and too sunny in your room
to leave the tent you've constructed
from old rope, wooden clothes pins,
and two black sheets. We sit Indian-style
on the mattress, palm to palm.
When we touch fingertips, you say
that you are a small boy; our hands,
the same size. We call ourselves *boy, girl, kid,*
never *man, woman.*

*The body is sacred;*
*no one should touch it unless you let them.*
You massage my foot, thumbs
kneading its tight sole. When you were eleven,
a boy, bigger than you, took you aside
and forced his darkness into you.
I was raised to accept brutality—
a feather duster slapping my legs
until I couldn't walk. We don't say more
since we can't imagine how the past
could be different. It has made us.
Our bodies carry the memories.

When the sun sets, we crawl
from the tent. You dance on a chair
under the Christmas lights
strung across the room, your brown hair
whirling in a coil, and you tell me
*you've come home—*

*You've come home.*

## Beginnings

Three days into the Chinese New Year Mother burns the rice
and Grandmother dreams her gray dream. I sit in a red dress,
taste tears as the walls begin to crumble. I've been in this house
less than two weeks and the light bulbs blow out
when I enter a room; the ashtray I set by the staircase explodes
as if struck by a mallet. In the backyard, you prime a canvas
and talk about Elena, the lover you wait for, so precious you say
you want to strangle her. You remind me I'm your roommate,
a body to warm you. Later you will crawl on top of my comforter,
brush your tongue over my neck, tell me no one treats me better.
Last Friday I salted a man's hand before we downed tequila.
He is the one I have avoided, a man who could love me,
love the soup reheating in the kitchen, the suitor for whom
the gods have accepted Grandmother's offering of boiled chicken
and whiskey. When I came home to you that night, the charm
you gave me was broken. The goddess escaped from the glass
which held her; two fingers missing from Buddha's hand.

## Sight

My best friend Charley was allergic to sunlight. I keep his photos
in milk cartons by the window, my little mole man under a hood
and baseball cap, only his librarian glasses showing. Charley and I
shared a room. He painted his eyes everywhere, told me to leave
mine open since I was the kid who fell down stairs, broke my back
in three places. I'd come home at night to valerian steeping in
a teapot, see neon eyes on shirts, pillows, and muddy work boots,
perfect cat-green irises dilating in the room's darkness. Once,
Charley painted barracuda eyes on the tips of my swim fins
so I wouldn't trip. Last winter, he was moving a broken piano
across the street—the church left it at the curb for free. He may
have slipped because of the weight, the frost, the dump truck.
The sun struck the chrome bumper, the plunging light caught
the boy full of eyes when he wasn't looking.

## Merritt

He's baggy pants dancing circles to world beat. "Hey, dorks
are cool. I don't write, but I think THOUGHTS!!!" He bangs
bongos sitting on laundry he hasn't washed in three years. Friends
say he can't add, but after three joints, his middle name is Jesus,
the healer, ever since the sitter snapped his noodle bone, and the
other children wrapped him in a shawl. "Don't trip on things,"
he says, turning over my left hand, seeing my fingertips older
than the palm. "You're not psychotic. Take me for instance:
last summer, I almost threw a woman through a wall.
You've heard the expression, seeing red? Well, roses are red."

## Of Soup and Love

In the winter when a young woman invites a young man for chowder,
he packs a bag. I had my knapsack ready. I worked as a museum guide.
Nadine was a guard telling people, *Don't touch.* I loved soup.
Two months later she was pregnant. I didn't want the baby, but fed her
bread and broth, held her head when she couldn't keep food down.
Her housemate told me Nadine planned the pregnancy. One morning,
I sat up in bed, my breath warming the air. Nadine was by the bathroom
door on her hands and knees. Moaning, hair stuck to her face, she scrubbed
blood off the white rug. She was hemorrhaging and scrubbing. I pulled
a long shirt over her. *A tubal pregnancy,* her doctor told me later.
A dark mass, bone and tissue, blocked the fallopian tube. That spring,
I held her and kissed the scar on her stomach, my strange little signature.

## Porcupine

She plowed her potato fields at night.
The local farmers whispered, *vampire.*
Sunlight drained her body, darkened
the butterfly rash across her cheeks.

She was 27 — illness had claimed her
spleen, gallbladder, & uterus,
& she could barely walk
or bathe herself—when the doctor
ran his finger down the test results
& told her, *Bad News. Lupus.*
*There is no cure.*

After her husband backed over a porcupine
in their driveway, she took in its red-eyed baby,
let the orphan gnaw on a broken-down shed
because it was greedy for the salty wood.

During the day, when the sun's rays
scorched the earth, she stayed inside,
vacuuming flies off the ceiling
& sketching for solace—
carving light into the dark
charcoal with her rubber eraser
& cracking the stiff joints
of her milk-blue hands.

She wanted visitors to call first,
but all her doors stood open — strange
pickaxes & wire strippers prickling
on the walls, Chinese lacquer,
wicker, baggies full of hair
that had fallen out — & sometimes
the porcupine woke from its bed of straw
& waddled indoors, raising
its barbed quills & swatting its tail
at the dogs that snapped at its head.

It would bristle up her leg
onto her lap. *Be real still,* she'd say
to the few friends who came by.
*Pet him in one direction only.*

## After the Bird

His Momma was sixteen when she had him, named him Jay
after the bird so he could be free. Saturday haze, hot summer
breaking, Jay packs shirts for Maine. He's why Grampy lives,
will live longer if he visits. Jay says he wants his family to die
so he can get on with his life. Once, he mixed sleeping pills
with rum, climbed up a treehouse. The drugs were time-released.
Grandpa, up at dawn in dungarees, slops the hogs, grafts three
different apples on one tree, doesn't come home till supper.
Jay imagines his grandpa so tired, he could sink in dirt and die.
Last night, he dreamt the family shopped for washing machines,
climbed into a dryer, were trapped spinning. On the farm,
Momma shoots a woodchuck tearing at her turnips, bites
her cuticles as the other woodchucks drag its body away.

## George Grosz "Suicide" 1916

In the window of an algae-green dive,
a topless prostitute, restless
and anemic, rotates
her sharp chin and Egyptian eyes
towards the tulip of profane blue
she holds to the dusky light
as the radiator clang
and muffled sounds
of fornicating neighbors
float through the room.
A pink invalid dwarf fidgets
near her torpedo breasts,
which are surely pointed
in the direction of a crime.
Outside, a man in a wilted suit
sprawls out, teeth clenched
into a lizard's smile,
hands loosening around
a silver cane. The suede blue derby
and gun have been tossed aside.
Through the city streets
the stalking vagrants and roaming wolves
stream in menstrual red, and on the corner
of the block, a dapper man, his eyes
downcast, dangles
from a bent lamppost.

# Bali

Life is just another method
of payment. You want to go back to Maine,
Indian farmboy in this big city, have your mother
spoon out comfort—
potato soup and baked yams—
talk to Grandpa about the iron plate
nailed to his brain during the war,
the vats of pig's blood outside the barn.

In four years, seven friends
committed suicide. This week another,
coming home for the holidays,
dies, the wide winter roads too slick
to hold his car in place. In Maine,
even the blueberries
and lobsters are stunted
by cold. After you left, forty people
followed you to California.

Now, the city's four corners are closing in.
It is Sunday and you are tired of fighting.
You tell me you want to go to Bali
where the day's most important event
is eating a big wedge of melon
against the haze of temples and smoky greens.

I sit in your room, know why
comfort can be as easy
as a trigger. In the three days since your friend's death,
you've covered every corner with your sculptures—
a blue baby hemorrhages on the table, rose and thorns
sprouting from his appendix, and a sperm angel
hangs, shaking from a clothes line.

## All My Life

my grandmother told me that good numbers
are born to me, and it is written
that I would never fail in life. Those who listen
always lead good lives, she said.

After my third attempt—Johnny Walker
and a bag of speed in a motel bathroom—
I wanted to believe her, moved into her home
under her protection, became
the embryo that hasn't seen light.
I wanted her words to carry me,
the tone of her voice vibrating
under my rib cage so I could live, grow
as invincible and brilliant as what she saw.

But then she said I was no longer young
and the lovers I chose would lead me
astray, fishing for the moon in a well.
Every year had to be the year
I would find the right man
with a good paycheck, a German car.
She wanted my lovers to leave
so their bad luck
could not block my way. I became afraid
of the ones who might stay, afraid of my choices
tainting the future, afraid of wanting to die.

Now I have moved away from her,
not wanting my life to be written.
This year I don't know if my lover is good
or bad. I am out of balance, my back moving
out of alignment, half my body numbed.

When my lover works my muscles,
pushes his fingertips along my spine,
I imagine he can puncture the skin,

dip his hand into the rib cage, take my heart
to the flame in the fireplace.
I am that much afraid, but I want to believe
I deserve my life and it is mine.

## Distance

You said she kept leaving you for a dentist, a gay prostitute
whose boyfriend has AIDS, and the short order cook
who bruised her. She needed someone pretty in her bed.
You'd always wait, stay home until she threw rocks to break
your window, begging to be let in. She taught you to want
bath water so hot you'd lose your senses. You are the one
who loves the most; the woman leaving when her body
heals. One night: gunshots and glass outside, another
woman's bra on the edge of your bed. I ask if you love me.
You wrap me in alpaca, bring me chamomile. *Once a lover,
always a lover,* you say. The following summer, you pack
condoms for your months away, tell me you are afraid
of the space you will come back to. I massage your back
so you can fall asleep. When you are gone, I drink tequila,
receive six letters, four phone calls. *You are the blessing
in my life,* you write. *You are a star.* I stay up, ask myself
if I am a blessing, peel off my clothes for a friend two days
before you come home.

## Wisdom

*You are blessed in life,* she says, touching a match
to a single spicy balsamic leaf, *but if you do not change
your direction, you will end up where you're going.* On her
kitchen counter, Ah-Pauh simmers bark and sweet oil
from parasitic trees. She asks the thousand-armed goddess
to throw protection over me—small fish my mother wants
to swallow. The hunter hollows a coconut, strung to a tree,
and pushes mango dumplings through the hole,
big enough for a monkey's open hand to slide through.
Too small for his clenched fist to pass. Buddha tells
the woman who carries her dead child on her hip,
*I know a medicine. You will need a handful of mustard
seed from a house where no child, husband, parent or
servant has died.* The woman walks miles, asking
house to house until there are no more houses. She lays
her child's body in a grove of trees, returns to Buddha.
*I have not brought the mustard seed. The living are few.*

## One Hundred and Eight Bald-Headed Buddhas

*I have things to show you*—old wrinkled Mr. Fook hobbles toward me
from the back of the Apothecary Gallery. I follow him through
the beaded curtain to an alley shack. His chihuahua is stretched out
on rosewood, her back paws tied down, tranced out on some
Chinese bowwow drug. *A bit closer . . .* he whispers. *Hold the forceps.*
In reality, one often assists in a hysterectomy as a form of greeting.
Her ovary comes free in my hand like a tiny pearl onion. *You can't
buy this from a flea market.* The old man laughs, hands me
a walnut carved with one hundred and eight bald-headed Buddhas.
*Inscribing the Lord's Prayer on a grain of rice is the nature of life.*
He turns to the figure of a man stalked by a tiger. *Now, he flees
from the Oldsmobile.* Then, he points at the scroll where a woman
is falling from a tree. *Now, it is the Golden Gate Bridge. Go home
and have your grandmother chart your fortune. I will tell you
if she is right.*

## Advice from a Former Lover, an Artist

You and I share a hunger for this perverse world.
We bear the mark of Cain, perpetually creating
to justify our ugliness. Since you married my friend
we haven't talked. Can I share some advice with you?
My wife and I have also tried to be like my parents:
to dig, plant, grow, and eat from the same soil together.
Well, Satan be praised. You don't have to trail
three steps behind your husband, and
we don't have to preserve turnips in brine.
The force of creation is not passive.
An artist chisels out form ruthlessly with full intent.
Show your obsessions like a marquee
on opening night. Pick the fruits ripe for you
and feast on the body. Ask him what he'd like
to sample first—red-fleshed blood oranges,
the translucent pulp pomegranates . . .
When the girl-next-door waves her supple scent
in front of his nose, and your tongue dances
like a flame, he may want a taste.
Sometimes, I look at my wife and say—
do you want to seduce another woman
while I watch? That's how I talk to my honey.
Other times, I tell friends my wife wants two men.
I blame it on her, but you know I love the act
of giving shape to desire, the inexplicable light
that lets us look into the secrets of others.

## Beneath the Surface

In a fish cleaning station near the equator,
off the coast of Africa, summer stretches
over the barracudas, their long mirrored-chrome
bodies heaped like eel fillets, slung jaws gaping,
red canine teeth exposed as if they still crave
meat and muscle. Even dead, they are a melancholy fish,
never satisfied, always wanting to bite off
more than they can chew, their curious white eyes
in a lidless showdown with an existence
beyond the visible. Maybe they are the spawn
of the serpent who prowled and tempted Eve,
cast into the saltwater. They are terrifying and defiant,
their pointed heads hammering towards the light,
waiting for the first sign of weakness. The fishermen
catch them hovering just beneath the surface.
What is it like to die with your eyes wide open
in the bright sun?

## Shaman

You rescue a music box from Goodwill because the old woman
died who bred dogs small enough to fit your palm. No skulls or
skeletons to polish, nail to drift wood, sell for rent money. Now
the music box. Something broken. You spent months painting
the little mummy man who lives inside, horse hair brushing his
stomach until a fetus formed. For him, you collect mink pelts
and American Beauties, true finds in a dumpster at daybreak.
You pull your own tooth to bring relief, shove in the bottom
drawer. When the box is opened, the metal music teeth refuse to
sit. The song skips and whines as the mummy man faces the
sky, as the mink longs for sleep, as he cocks one eye through a
hole in the lid. It isn't even a dream; these notes climb through
the open mouth. You hear the dead keep singing.

## Peel

The fool stands on a mountain, world spread before him. Priscilla, a Roman
family name, means ancient wisdom. The sphinx seized travelers on the road,
asked them a riddle, ate those who cannot answer. Man is the answer. Under-
stand your humanity or life could destroy you. If you don't see the unpleasant
truth about yourself, you are unaware of what you have to offer the world.
Priscilla Alden in *The Courtship of Miles Standish* says, "John, why don't you
speak for yourself."

Priscilla, the Aries Firehorse, where "i" is primary, the wood under fire,
the fire behind flames. The fire in the heart giving voice. 李 Lee.
The 子 child under the 木 tree. Child, fool, the first and final path
on the tree of life. The crown of wisdom, the wisdom of the crown.
The Kabbalists said those whose primary vowel is "i" enter the world
to build a life like a tree's. Roots in earth, limbs stretching towards heaven.

Percy, Percival, Parsifal. Eating salmon wounds the Grail King. He suffers,
cannot drink from the healing Grail. Percy, the fool who slumbers in sun-rot
clothes, restores the Fisher King. Percy who asks, "whom does the Grail serve?"
In the Tang dynasty, the Emperor Lee rewarded his warriors with his last name.
Loyalty, their heart in the center, the heart in the right place.

Cilla, Scilla, Scylla: Circe poisons the pond Scylla bathes in. Her body sprouted
serpents and dog's heads. She stood rooted to rock. Risc, risk: the possibility
of suffering harm or loss. Prometheus stole fire, is chained to rock at the mercy
of birds that tear at his liver. Regeneration and resurrection, you must overcome
your lower nature. The decayed tooth must be pulled to bring the body relief.

Lee Quan Yi, the Chinese name. 君 Quan. A polite scholar or official.
怡 Yi. Happy and tranquil. 口 the open mouth in Quan and Yi.
If you are a scholar, what you say is important. In a fairy tale, the parts
of the body battle over which has more power. Only the milk of a lion
can cure the dying emperor. A young scholar volunteers to save him:
his eyes spot the den, his ears listen for stirring, his hands milk the sleeping
animal, his legs carry him to safety. When the scholar brings the milk to the
emperor, the tongue takes control. "I have brought the sacred milk of a hedge-
hog." The emperor orders, "hang him and let his tongue hang out." The tongue

scoffs at the other body parts, "With one word, I can undo anything." The open mouth, Peh, the Tower in the tarot, the Tower of Babel shaken to the roots.

Janus from Jane, the middle name. The god of gates and doorways, two faces look in opposite directions. To live is to search many paths to discover a fruitful one. Jane: God's gracious gift. A present wrapped to conceal its contents. Peel the layers of an onion to its heart. Lee is eel spelled backwards.

Snake shedding skin.

# Fortune

Every year on the cusp of old and new,
Grandmother kneels in front of the fireplace
with her Tung Shu and bookmarks,
tosses five quarters onto brick.
She watches the order
in which they fall, scratches my name
with her brittle fingernail into the book's margin
when she has matched
their sequence to a fortune.

This year was a good year, next will be better,
she always tells me after studying the characters.
The warrior who has won the battle
stands at a crossroad,
and his horse is hungry.
The carp tries to leap
the high wall, its scales
a blistering glare. The fisherman
catches the prize pelican
with an oyster in its long beak.
The kirin, half tiger, half dragon,
enters the forbidden city.

Year after year, she wants my fortunes
to drag me toward the coming year, but
how can I be as certain as Grandmother
that my life is good? The warrior has won a battle,
but does he complete his journey
if he has no horse, no food? Is the carp's leap
transcendent or defiant? Which am I—
fisherman, oyster, or pelican?
And the kirin, the long-awaited prince—
to what political state is he born, and
what does it mean to be a prince and a woman?

## The Marker

for Choy Sing Lee, my great-grandfather

*Leaves fall to the ground where the roots are buried.*

Ten thousand miles from Say Ah, Canton,
your great-grandchildren gather, backs
toward the east, unable to read the characters
on your headstone. We lay out a picnic
of roast pork and dim sum, burn gold prayer papers
for your well-being and abundance in afterlife.

Great-grandfather, under the red Delta blaze,
you picked pears and tomatoes from Lodi
and Walnut Grove, harvest to harvest, climbing
the roads where the sky seemed out of reach.
At night, in a bunkhouse, twelve to a room,
you ate wet bean curd over rice gruel, sent money
so your family could buy oyster sauce and shoes.

You wrote the family about your cousin,
the big city merchant so blessed with wealth,
he had no sense. He did not build a home
in the village; his family didn't return
to clear the weeds from his grave.
You vowed you would be smarter.

With money you sent, your wife built
the biggest mansion in Say Ah
for your retirement: thirty-six windows,
a living room stretching the length of the road,
but you did not come home. Your heart
broke when you read:
Your wife, force-fed buckets of water,
was dragged into the white sun to dry.

Your daughter asks, how could her husband,
handcuffed, have hanged himself?
You died in America, huddled in a bathroom,
underwear coiled at your ankles,
the letter tucked in your pocket.

That was the summer Communists pounded
the iron gates, their voices ringing
*leeches bleeding the poor.* Your sons escaped
the squad of guns, their black trunk weighted
with photos of the dead, and your descendants
took root in San Francisco. Visitors to Say Ah
tell your sons about rotting floors, windows smashed
by rocks. During Ch'ing Ming, each May,
your great-grandchildren rake thistles and snails
that cover your grave, lug water up a hill
to scrub the marker, set it back in place.

## China

On our dining table, every dish is a dime-store pattern:
blue dandelions, red nasturtiums, the entire stack,
a small legacy won in a 1959 coin toss
by Lealand, the uncle with the long arms
and legs, who pitched penny after penny
at a parking lot carnival until his pockets
were emptied of everything, but lint and luck.

My family wouldn't buy Emporium bowls
thick like heads of cabbage or soup spoons
holding hand-painted water lilies;
our plates, chipped and resounding,
clatter at every feast. In America,
we acquired what was necessary:
some English to earn a living, cotton
for dull work, enough noodles for a long life.

My father and uncles fled China
with a black leather trunk, four wool sweaters,
and proud photographs of their two-story mansion.
They rented on Mason, Alfred's Steakhouse clanging
all night below. Great-Uncle's wife
donated a lazy susan, mini Bora Bora
pitchforks, and wooden bowls, rancid
from salad oil—whatever she couldn't unload
at her yard sale. Sundays, she invited
her nephews to hang coats, change diapers,
and serve finger sandwiches, told guests,
*ignore those farmboys, too stupid to say yes or no.*

The boys didn't tell her about the jars of jade
or the "big house," its pond
swimming with yolk-eating carp.
They studied calculus and chemistry
and worked after school, eighty-five cents an hour,
pouring coffee at Mee Heung Bakery
and ironing pleats in sweat shops

towards a new life: chicken and fresh fish
every day, wonton noodle soup and television
at midnight, Grace Kelly on weekends. *When I get off the boat,
America is a beautiful country,* my father says
as he watches Uncle Lealand, the organoleptic specialist, dish up
the leftover black bean lobster for his cats.

## The Web of the Dream Catcher

~

Is the house of the spider fragile?

I used to read aloud
to my great grandmother on the porch swing. She couldn't
see, and she loved the tale about a spider that saves her
friend by weaving words in her web. When I became tired,
I would lie across my great grandmother's lap, and she
would cradle my head and sing.

~

My mother didn't want holy water to touch our foreheads
or river water to soak our clothes. Our hearts didn't need
purification. One day we would find our own way
into the world of spirits.

When we were fifteen, my friend and I dragged three logs
into the pit behind my mother's house and stood them
against each other to form a peak. We sat molding clay,
the thick earth absorbing water, our fingers penetrating
its shapelessness. Later, we threw the objects down
into the coals to fire. We sifted through the ash a few days
later, gathered toys, tiny seed pots, and people.

~

The weaver sat by the loom, legs tucked beneath her.
I looked at her cloak of rippling water and asked how long
it would take to complete. Her answer let me know
she would be there until all existence has connected
like the great strands of a web.

She was warping her loom when she told me her
nightmare. *You are cradling a baby with a blurry face.*
*When I run to you, you have eyes on your neck.* She pulled
clouds from the sky, passed them over and under
the long threads.

~

I splashed my face with water. The mirror showed, on my neck,
two perfect almond-shaped blemishes.

Behind me a wrenching sound and a *ping, ping, ping.*
The nails in the window frame backed out and fell
to the floor. Both windows opened and a wind circled
my head. Posters and paintings tore from the walls,
my pet bird spiraled towards the ceiling. *Am I in the dream
or is the dream in me?* The wind was passing beyond
the threads of time.

~

My head pounded and she held me, rocked me back
and forth. The weaver started to hum. The melody
soothed me; the sun flooded my body. I hummed
with her. *What were you singing?* She remembers
part of a dream: three burning pyramids. Two people
sitting in the center.

She wraps the wool and silk shawl around me,
says it is like putting on God.

# The Kiss

It is the spring my grandfather would die,
the supply truck sitting by the gate,
oxygen tanks in the garage,
diaper boxes stacked by his door.

You have the keys
to your grandparents' house—spiral brick
staircase, pastel walls,
high ceilings. We enter through the garage,
the realtor's lock on the front door.
When you were young, you ate here:
plates of lamb with prunes and honey, glasses of robust red.
On Fridays, baked chicken with pecans.

You point at the Polaroids
tacked in each room, murky
like small aquariums with seaweed, shells,
and invisible fish. *Oppa is like that,*
*pictures on the walls to show buyers*
*what the house looked like furnished.*

You wouldn't tell me why
he left the cut-glass chandelier hanging
in the dining room. What you say instead:
*there used to be parties, bowls of cashews,*
*sliced oranges, dark chocolates,*
*hot baths, riddles to keep me*
*awake at nights.*

In your grandparents' bedroom,
I drop my purse on the floor and walk around.
You pick it up, pull its strap over your shoulder,
bend down and kiss me. There are stories
about people making love in empty houses,
but this isn't about that. We stand awkward,
the emptiness all around us.

We drive afterwards to the supermarket to buy
mints and soda, pass a newspaper stand on fire,
Bob Dylan blaring on the radio.
*She's an artist, she don't look back.*

## North Yarmouth

an ordinary town of great sorrow.

Your parents raised five pairs
of bored little hands to milk cows,
pull weeds. You had a younger sister

once. She was twelve, walking
home from school in a red
afternoon, heavy as poached game,
when a man dragged her into the underbrush.
They did not find her body. After that, it was harder:
a family with a hole in its heart. She was like

your mother, the shadows bleeding
over hard cheekbones
like a turbulent dream,
the oiled hair, black as figs. Your mother
often did the unexpected, came home
from the beauty parlor with hair wrapped in newspaper
like a bundle of fish, planted it in the yard. Buried finger
and toe nails. Baby hair
from a locket. All things from earth

return to the earth. You left for the army, three years
scraping your soul across Germany, hauling
a canvas bag. *Ein Bier, bitte.* The first girl
you loved wanted you to beat her up. Sometimes lying

in bed with you, I wonder why you are so kind. I've watched
you wrap the cat in a blanket and kiss its face. Sometimes
cats have bad dreams about being human.

# Rock 'n' Roll Odyssey

At night his penis is a small Cyclops, half-asleep,
as he drifts back into his band—the Blots on
the Stone-Deaf Pig record label, who drank
bath water by the shotglass full, Boston 80s
Punk, anything to please his goat, Baptist boy
in trashed black trousers and Beatles boots,
his electric guitar ripping into it heavy
like a heated chainsaw, nothing dickless,
none of that ca-tink-ca-tink-ca bar crap.
He knew only a cult band can have integrity.
*The band was so poor, we ate bread ends*
*from the Greek deli and ketchup soup.*
He didn't want to sell out to success
on their way to becoming gods.
The waitresses, *them sirens,* thought
he was a sonofabitch, *Bette Davis eyes*
*and Belinda Carlisle's thighs, gotta remember*
*not to catch the knife when it falls,* he says,
*See?* The only cock cooking at an all-girls school,
it was a good time to be had. *Yup.* LSD and he
wrapped the car around a campus tree, but Hell
the penguins liked him. He served their meals first.
Totaling the Mustang wasn't as bad
as when he sold blood for $30,
got mugged outside the clinic.
The holy penguins couldn't waddle
fast enough to save his ass.

## The Duckman at Redwood Shores

Every day before the world falls apart,
before the flood of grieving begins, before the office workers
ask him *how big is a small bowl of soup,* before his new helper
can drop another heavy pan on his foot, the man
in the green smock, stained
with fish oil, steps out to the pond.

He carries a styrofoam container
for his wife like the burden
of his heart. Depression
has grayed her teeth. He wants
to take care of his little baby,
who won't let him teach her how
to drive a car or cook a simple casserole.
At night, she talks in her sleep
about the parasites
which swim behind her eyes.

When he arrives at the table, he strokes
her cheek, *eat it now while it's still hot, honey,*
but the ducks hurry towards him, orange-rubber feet
pattering up the cement path, ruddy quacks
descending the scale. He rips apart
a wheat roll and the two loaves
of French. The brown-mottled females
gargle, feeding out of his hands, careful
not to peck his fingers. His wife picks
at the pesto, sun-dried tomatoes,
and caramelized onions which lie in a pile.

He tells his wife, he can't wait for them
to have babies. He knows they can be so soft.
When he was a boy, he owned
a little food duck, carried her in his jacket
one mile to the pond. She learned
how to swim, nuzzling for seeds
from the pond's muddy bottom, startling

the clouds of fish. He often watched
as the duck waddled home, the other birds
clapping their wings above her.
She never learned to fly.

## Driving with My Third Eye

### 1

Talking to God wasn't my objective
when I crawled behind the wheel,
but I needed someone to point out the brakes,
so Lily, my driving teacher, decided to show me
how to pray. *What's that piece of jade?*
*Who is Kuan Yin?*
*Why talk to an enlightened being*
*when you could talk directly to the Head Honcho?*
When I whipped around a policeman
on a horse, she held her palm
over my head to open channels.
Her hand blocked my view, but I sensed
a wave of heat. My head was getting hot.
Maybe she was praying for everyone.

### 2

Cleaning house after her messy divorce,
my tarot reader gave me her crystal ball,
advised me to scrub it with sea salt.
At the market, I got lost in the BBQ aisle.
When I asked the plump coupon woman,
*where's the salt,* she yanked a quartz wand
from under her T-shirt and shook it
in my face. *You're not ready to open yourself*
*to the world of shadows. You let the wrong kind in.*
*That's why you have so many nasal infections.*

### 3

A long time ago, my grandmother and grandfather
were attendants to the Emperor of Heaven.
They broke the Emperor's teacups.
The Empress sentenced them to marriage
on Earth. They didn't have a happy union,
but understood why they must endure.

### 4

My therapist, Amy, goes into a trance
and starts eating pistachios. She tells me
I was born to a woman attracted
to shopping and meat ball recipes, and
my grandmother wonders if my kidneys
grew in right. I can't give her an answer,
but Grandma and I trade readings, check up
on each other twice a week with cards and coins.
Amy pictures her as my drinking buddy
in a previous life, the two of us nudging elbows
in a thatched hut, sharing our bag of remedies
over whiskey and boiled peanuts.


### 5

After years posing as a technical writer
and passing, I sat penciling bubble
after bubble of a Myers-Briggs personality test.
Later, the result exposed that I was
the only Shirley MacLaine/Mother Teresa
in the room. I asked the instructor to direct me
to my path. *Oh my.* She answered. *It's inherited.*
*The seers, the prophets,*
*the poets of this world.*
I told her my father is an accountant,
but my grandmother's a fortune teller.
She told me sometimes it skips a generation.

# Instructions

1.  To consecrate oil, face the east.
    Watch the sun spark the bottle.
    Ask the sun for copper cords to ground
    your feet. In the evening, face the west.
    Shine the moon through the bottle.
    Ask the moon to burn your sails,
    change your direction.

2.  To clear your light, anoint
    your forehead. Draw your finger across
    your neck where all confusion lies.
    Touch the bottoms and tops of your feet.
    Your presence is egg-shaped, radiating
    three-feet around you. If the light extends
    beyond the room, call it back.
    It has no business in someone else's space.

3.  Charging the spell with intent
    is like shooting an arrow. Focus, pull, shoot:
    your consciousness is the target.
    Imagine the blue flame flickering.
    When you release your thoughts,
    blank your mind. Throw the spell
    into the light. Ask his heart for justice.

4.  To gain separation, soak a mayonnaise jar
    in warm water, scrape off the bar code.
    Write your name and his name on a piece of paper.
    Add half apple cider vinegar, half piss.
    Seal in a paper bag. Hide
    in the darkest shelf for a month. Discard.
    You are a wolf marking territory, claiming
    yourself back.

## At the Wonton Monkee

My husband, the ex-army mess cook
from Maine, doesn't fight
the neighborhood grub, doesn't expect much
in the way of good truck-stop coffee,
small talk, or accurate translations
from the blunt-faced waitresses who hurry
customers & order for them. As he cleans
his chopsticks with tea, the way
I showed him, Iron Goddess of Mercy
stripping their sticky shine, I muscle
him to try the blackboard special—
fish bladders bubbling
in a clay pot—to break out
of his sweet & sour rut. After all,
our children will be half Chinese.
He eyes scaly pike plucked
from the live tank, orders the #34,
Happy Chicken—Mild. At the far end,
the chow-splattered fat guy, whose face
decorates the greasy menu, chops slabs
of roasted suckling & cleaves open
the pearled flesh of an octopus, tossing it,
hot & bothered, to ooze its briny ink
onto a bed of rice. It's a sinus-clearing
classic only we Cantonese can stomach,
not honest like steak, served as bloody
as you like. *The only things*
*the Chinese won't eat are rocks,*
my husband comments, poking
at his chicken cubes, crimson red
& more sour than sweet.

## How to Stuff an Eggplant

For once, forget Bongo's Burger Joint
& thank El Nino for the pulsing hillsides.
Go to the farmer's market & choose
a glossy eggplant, just-harvested,
that shimmers back at you.
At home, rub its purple skin with dark oil
carried up from a cool cellar.
Broil the eggplant inches from the heat.
Carefully scoop the spongy white flesh,
leaving walls thick enough to hold.
Fill the hollow with walnuts, tangy feta,
& pomegranate seeds. Pack a basket.
Walk slowly along a trail winding
through wildflowers, a riot of color
down to the beach. Don't hurry.
Scatter the fat sparrows as you shake out
your picnic cloth stained with grass
from last summer. Place the eggplant,
warm & full, in the curve
of your lover's palm. Watch him
savor the soft succulent meat.
Dig your toes into the sand.
Let the mingled juices drip
onto the blanket while he nibbles.

## Meditation at the Sushi Boat Place

Don't judge anyone
the way you judge your mother.
Forget ambition. Tangle in someone else's
sheets at least twice a week.
It doesn't matter if he's not there
as long as it makes sense. Sleep until one,
make love until three, order in Szechuan noodles
with chunky peanut butter. Believe you're immortal
until you die. Never live with your parents
a second time. Never eat anything
bigger than your face. Be free, but not
too free. Don't sleep with anyone who flosses
his teeth with your hair; no one loves
a plucked ostrich. Repeat to yourself
affirmations don't work.
The Almighty doesn't want you
to sound like a leaf-wrapped parrot,
baking in hot ashes. Always mix wasabi
with ice cream made of green tea.

## George, My Husband, Didn't Expect to Live in San Francisco

The full moon beams as if it had eaten
blue cheese & burped into the sky.
The pasta trucks rumble down
the Great Highway. Our cat, petite
in her black sealskin coat, claws at the ghost
of a mouse in our dark wood kitchen.
I can almost taste the *pappardelle con*
*il ragu di fegatini* as my husband, the refugee
from Mattawamkeag, Maine, sways
in his plaid boxer shorts, stirring
his chicken-liver sauce. The evening smells
the way the cheese felt when it melted.
It's in the mood for love. George laughs
since he didn't expect to live in San Francisco,
ten years after seeing the bridge collapse.
The moon won't eat cheese. Tom Waits,
who keeps an eye on life, chokes up
a melody— *outside, another yellow*
*moon has punched a hole in the nighttime.*
The black ink of my life keeps writing
on the right squid of my brain.
The cat screams in Cantonese,
telepathically, again Big Pris, unsettled
by her migraine, stands on her head.
She'll have quintuplets by Cesarean section
when she's 41, & they'll frolic in red
rain slickers & tiny duck shoes. These hip babies
will love asparagus spiced Eritrean &
George'll have to feed them milkshakes
to make them hungry. *Mutt-ye ho? M-goi, tai ha.*
*What's good? Let me have a look.*
Baby Cat slurps the sauce,
twirling the angel hair in her paws.
The moon blows a raspberry at the comets
as they somersault through the night.
George & Pris turn off the light

& pull the blankets for bed. The fog horns
groan & the cat wants to build
a bonfire & sauté her littleneck clams.

## Burnt Offerings: Mother's Day at the Lee's, 1999

On Mother's Day, Dad invited the mechanic, his wife, and three
small children, to resuscitate his '76 Nova, which was the color
of a wrinkled orange and spilling more oil from every crevice
than the Exxon Valdez into the neighbors' flat calm driveways.
Dad only drove it from one side to the other to avoid street cleaners.
It was his first car, and my maternal grandmother, who died
years ago, had lent him the money to buy it. We were setting
the table with Szechwan from Mike's Chinese when the car burst
into flames. Thirty Chinese and one half-Cherokee streamed toward
the burning Nova. George, my husband, yelled at them to stop
pointing the garden hose at the gasoline fire, but everyone
screamed back in Cantonese. No one wanted to call 911.
The Chinese don't like making a scene, but it's OK
for the car to ignite other nearby cars, its flames traveling
slowly along the oil slicks. Auntie Claire suggested we pour
a box of baking soda on the fire. While Dad tried to retrieve
his stash of lucky red envelopes from the glove compartment,
twelve firefighters shattered the car windows with their axes.
Afterwards we ate. Then George and I stepped out for a smoke
and watched the neighbors celebrate the rise in property values
as the tow truck dragged away the charred hulk.

## Dim Sum & Then Some

At the Eight Immortals—where the Lee kids are known
to sprawl in front of dim sum carts, checking out
the shark fin dumplings & ham ha ngau yuk chow fun—
the owner prefers to seat us in the banquet room upstairs.
Grandma loves her grandchildren, doesn't want us to marry
& move out of state! The boys pat her head, sputtering
Chinglish & adjusting tones until they hit the mark.
On special occasions, when Canadian half-relatives visit,
second uncle's lanky second son, Ellison, tapes styrofoam
cups to his chest, piles waist-length hair on top of his head,
& grooves like a drag queen waitress in heat. If our blind
Grandpa were alive, his one blue eye would try to stare
down our antics. Last year I married & now I'm chewing
the fat at the grown-up table, talking about my 401K.
I miss the steamed bun fights, the 11-kid stadium wave
around our table, & the puppet show—chicken & duck heads
stuck on chopsticks, pecking at each other, their pink napkin
dresses trailing in the soy sauce.

"Down": The line, "I know you're wrong you're not that strong" is from the song "One More Try" by George Michael.

"Wisdom": Ideas and lines were adapted from *Legacy of the Heart* by Wayne Muller.

"Peel": Ideas or lines were adapted from *The Sacred Power in Your Name* by Ted Andrews, *The Spirit of the Chinese Character* by Barbara Aria and Russell Eng Gon, *Bulfinch's Mythology* by Thomas Bulfinch, *The Fisher King and the Handless Maiden* by Robert A. Johnson, *Seventy-Eight Degrees of Wisdom* (I and II) by Rachel Pollack, *The Witches Tarot* and *The Witches Qabalah* by Ellen Cannon Reed, *The Last Word on First Names* by Linda Rosenkrantz and Pamela Redmond Satran, and "The Great Debate," retold by Peninnah Schram in *Parabola: The Magazine of Myth & Tradition,* Volume 20, Number 2.

"George, My Husband, Didn't Expect to Live in San Francisco": The line, "outside, another yellow moon has punched a hole in the nighttime" is from the song "Downtown Train" by Tom Waits.

The *California Poetry Series* celebrates the great diversity of aesthetics, culture, geography, and ethnicity of the state by publishing work by poets with strong ties to California. Books within this series are published quarterly. Malcolm Margolin of Heyday Books is the publisher; Joyce Jenkins of Poetry Flash is editor.

An advisory board of prominent poets and cultural leaders has been assembled to encourage and support California poetry through this book series. These include Alfred Arteaga, Chana Bloch, Christopher Buckley, Marilyn Chin, Karen Clark, Wanda Coleman, Gillian Conoley, Peter Coyote, Jim Dodge, Lawrence Ferlinghetti, Jack Foley, Jewelle Gomez, Robert Hass, Jane Hirshfield, Fanny Howe, Lawson Inada, Jaime Jacinto, Diem Jones, Stephen Kessler, William Kistler, Carolyn Kizer, Steve Kowit, Dorianne Laux, Philip Levine, Genny Lim, Suzanne Lummis, Lewis MacAdams, David Mas Masumoto, David Meltzer, Deena Metzger, Carol Muske-Dukes, Jim Paul, Kay Ryan, Richard Silberg, Gary Snyder, Dr. Kevin Starr, David St. John, Sedge Thomson, Alan Williamson, and Gary Young.

*California Poetry Series* books are available at bookstores nationwide or by subscription ($40.00/year). For more information:
Heyday Books
P.O. Box 9145
Berkeley, CA 94709
phone: 510.549.3564 fax: 510.549.1889
e-mail: roundhouse@heydaybooks.com
www.heydaybooks.com

C A L I F O R N I A   P O E T R Y   S E R I E S